the beaco

(Revised Edition)

Book Five

Briar Rose

By **James H. Fassett**

Series Editor (Revised Edition)
Francis Fanthome

USING THIS BOOK

Briar Rose is intended for children who are ready to pass beyond the standard of achievement for infant school reading represented by *Careful Hans* (Book Four Stage of Beacon Reading). In content, arrangement, and vocabulary this book is adapted to their needs. Progression in content is marked by the inclusion of legendary tales with some of the well-loved folk and fairy tales. In arrangement, paragraphs tend to become longer and, instead of being confined to one idea, or fact, may contain several. In vocabulary, out of a total of 1715 different words, 949 have not been met in the main readers of the previous Stages, and the number of new words introduced is just about twice as large as that in *Careful Hans*. The justification for this increase in vocabulary lies, of course, in the ripening of the child's phonic powers as he has moved from stage to stage in Beacon Reading and in the growth of his reading 'sense'.

The new Phonic Group Tables and Pronunciation Exercises at the end of this book are important. A few minutes spent on them daily will reflect favourably on the children's speech, spelling, and powers of quick and accurate word recognition. In these tables, for the first time in the Beacon Plan, there are included words with a vowel combination or an eccentricity of pronunciation which has not previously been studied in a formal Phonic Group Table because examples are not sufficient to warrant their inclusion in a Table of their own. Because of this it will be all the more evident to teachers that if children are forewarned through practice on these tables of some of the anomalies of English pronunciation which they have to meet as they read more and more, they will be forearmed when the encounter actually takes place.

© James H. Fassett 1923
Revised Edition 2002

Illustrations: Mohan Singh
Layout and design: Textsure
Printed in India by Gopsons Papers Ltd

IMP 30 29 28 27 26 25

CONTENTS

Title	Source	Page
The Shoemaker and the Elves	English Folk Tale	5
The Wolf and the Seven Young Kids	William and Jacob Grimm	11
Tom Thumb	English Fairy Tale	19
Cinderella	English Fairy Tale	27
The Four Friends	William and Jacob Grimm	33
Mother Frost	William and Jacob Grimm	43
Why the Bear's Tail is Short	German Folk Tale	53
Rumpelstiltskin	William and Jacob Grimm	57
The Golden Touch	Greek Myth	69
The Bell of Atri	German Folk Tale	77
Escape from Red Indians	American Tradition	83
Dick Whittington	English Legend	93
Briar Rose	William and Jacob Grimm	103
The Baker Boys and the Bees	German Legend	113
The First Wife's Wedding Ring	J.H. Ewing	119
David and Goliath	Adapted from the Bible	131

THE SHOEMAKER AND THE ELVES

sew   bought   already

A shoemaker and his wife lived in a little house on the edge of a wood.

They were very, very poor, and each day they grew poorer and poorer.

At last there was nothing left in the house but leather for one pair of shoes.

"I will cut out this last pair of shoes," the shoemaker said to his wife.

"Tomorrow I will sew them and peg them."

So he cut out the leather and left it on his bench.

The next morning he went into his shop to make the shoes.

What did he see?

A pair of shoes, all nicely made and ready to be sold.

The stitches were so fine and the shoes so well made that they were quickly sold.

With the money the poor shoemaker bought leather for two pairs of shoes.

Then he said to his wife, "I will cut out the leather for two pairs of shoes.

"Tomorrow I will sew them and peg them."

So he cut out the leather for the shoes and left it on the bench.

The next morning when he went into his shop to make the shoes, what did he find?

Yes, there were two pairs of shoes already made.

The work was so well done that those shoes also were sold very quickly.

With the money the poor shoemaker bought enough leather for four pairs of shoes.

Those he also cut out and left upon his bench.

The next morning he found four pairs of beautiful shoes, all well made.

And so it went on and on. Instead of being a very poor shoemaker, he became a very rich shoemaker.

His shoes were so well made that even the queen herself wore them.

At last the shoemaker said to his wife, "We must find out who makes the shoes."

So one bright moonlight night they hid behind a curtain, where they could watch the bench and not be seen.

Just on the stroke of midnight, two little elves jumped through the window.

They went skipping and dancing up to the bench.

Sitting cross-legged they took up the leather and began to work.

How their needles flew back and forth, back and forth!

How their little hammers beat rap-a-tap-tap, rap-a-tap-tap!

Almost before the shoemaker and his wife could think, the work was all done.

The two tiny elves ran about, skipping and dancing, skipping and dancing.

Then, whisk ! Quick as a wink, they were gone.

The next morning the good shoemaker said to his wife, "What can we do for those dear little elves?"

"I should like very much to make some clothes for them," said his wife. "They were almost naked."

"If you will make their coats, I will make them some shoes," said the shoemaker. "Their little feet were bare."

When the clothes and shoes were ready, they were put upon the bench.

The shoemaker and his wife again hid behind the curtain.

Just as before, when the clock struck twleve, in jumped the tiny elves.

They went skipping and dancing, skipping and dancing, to their work.

They saw the little coats, the tiny stockings, and the neat little shoes.

They clapped their hands for joy.

Then, slipping on their clothes, they skipped, hand in hand, out of the window.

The shoemaker and his wife never saw the little elves again, but after that night, good luck seemed always to be with them.

THE WOLF AND THE SEVEN YOUNG KIDS

    rough   chalk   scissors

There was once an old goat who had seven little kids. She loved them all as much as any mother ever loved her children.

One day the old goat wished to go into the woods to get food for her kids.

Before she started she called them all to her and said,

"Dear children, I am going into the woods.

"Now do not open the door while I am away.

"If the old wolf should get into our hut, he would eat you all up, and not a hair would be left.

"You can easily tell him by his rough voice and his black feet."

"Dear mother," cried all the young kids, "we will be very careful not to let the old wolf in.

"You need not think of us at all, for we shall be quite safe."

So the old goat went on her way into the dark woods.

She had not been gone long when there came a loud <u>rap</u> at the door, and a voice cried,

"Open the door, my dear children.
"I have something here for each of you."

But the young kids knew by the rough voice that this was the old wolf.

So one of them said, "We shall not open the door. Our mother's voice is soft and gentle. Your voice is rough. You are a wolf."

The old wolf ran away to a shop, where he ate a piece of white chalk to make his voice soft.

Then he went back to the goat's hut and rapped at the door.

He spoke in a soft voice and said,

"Open the door for me, my dear children. I am your mother."

But the oldest little goat thought of what his mother had said.

"If you are our mother, put your foot on the window sill, that we may see it."

When the wolf had done this, all the little goats cried out. "No, you are not our mother. We shall not open the door. Our mother's feet are white and yours are black. Go away; you are the wolf."

Then the wolf went to the baker's, and said to him, "Mr. Baker, put some flour on my foot, for I have hurt it."

The baker was so afraid of the wolf that he did as he was told.

Then the wicked wolf went to the goat's house again and said, "Open the door, dear children, for I am your mother."

"Show us your foot," said the little kids.

So the wolf put his one white foot on the window sill.

When the little kids say that it was white, they thought this was really their mother, and they opened the door.

In jumped the ugly old wolf, and all the little kids ran to hide themselves.

The first hid under the table, the second in the bed, the third in the oven, the fourth in the kitchen, the fifth in the cupboard, the sixth under the washtub, and the seventh, who was the smallest of all, in the tall clock.

The wolf quickly found and gobbled up all but the youngest, who was in the clock.

Then the wolf, who felt sleepy, went out and lay down on the green grass.

Soon he was fast asleep.

Not long after this the old goat came home from the woods.

Ah, what did she see! The house door was wide open; the tables and chairs were upset.

The washtub was broken in pieces, and the bed was tipped over.

"Where are my children?" cried the poor goat.

At last she heard a little voice crying, "Dear mother, here I am in the tall clock."

The old goat helped the little goat out.

Soon she learned how the wolf had eaten her dear children.

Then she went out of the hut, and there on the grass lay the wolf sound asleep.

As the goat looked at the wicked old wolf, she thought she saw something jumping about inside him.

"Ah," she said, "it may be that my poor children are still alive."

So she sent the little kid into the house for a pair of scissors and a needle and some thread.

She quickly cut a hole in the side of the wicked old wolf.

At the first snip of the scissors, one of the kids stuck out his head.

As the goat cut, more and more heads popped out.

At last all six of the kids jumped out upon the grass. They went hopping and skipping about their mother.

Then the old goat said to them, "Go and bring me some large stones from the brook."

The seven little kids ran off to the brook and soon came back with seven large stones.

They put these stones inside the wicked old wolf.

The old goat sewed up the wolf's side so gently and quietly that he did not wake up or move.

When at last the wicked wolf did wake up, the great stones inside him made him feel very heavy.

He was thirsty too, so he walked down to the brook to drink.

The stones were so heavy that they tipped him over the edge of the bank into the deep water, and he was drowned.

TOM THUMB

forest   people   reins   suit   fought

In the days of King Arthur, there lived a wise man named Merlin.

He knew all the fairies and where they lived. Even the fairy queen was a friend of his.

Once, while he was travelling, night overtook him in a deep forest.

He rapped at the door of a small cottage and asked for some food.

Merlin looked so hungry and poor that the farmer and his wife took pity on him.

They not only gave him a bowl of milk with some brown bread, but they said he might stay through the night.

Merlin saw that, in spite of their pleasant cottage, both the farmer and his wife were very sad.

"Why are you sad?" asked Merlin.

"You seem to have a good farm, a pleasant cottage, and many things to make you happy."

"Ah!" said the woman, "We are unhappy because we have no child.

"I should be the happiest woman in the world if I had a son. Why, even if he were no bigger than my husband's thumb, we should love him dearly."

"That would be indeed a very strange kind of child," said Merlin, "but I hope you may have your wish."

Now Merlin was on his way to call on the queen of the fairies.

When he came to her castle the next day, he told the fairy queen the wish of the farmer's wife.

The queen of the fairies said, "The good woman shall have her wish. I will give her a son no larger than her husband's thumb."

Soon after this good farmer's wife had a son. He was, indeed, just the size of his father's thumb. People came from far and wide to see the tiny boy.

One day the fairy queen and some other fairies came to see him.

The queen kissed the little boy and named him Tom Thumb.

Each of the other fairies made Tom a gift.

He had a shirt made of silk from a spider's web, a coat of thistledown, a hat made from the leaf of an oak, tiny shoes made from a mouse's skin, and many other gifts besides.

Tom never grew any larger than a man's thumb, but he could do many clever tricks.

One day his mother was mixing a pudding.

Tom leaned over the edge of the bowl to see how it was made.

He slipped, and in he went, head first.

His mother did not see him fall, and kept stirring and stirring the pudding.

Tom could not see or hear, but he kicked and kicked inside the pudding.

The pudding moved and tossed about.

His mother was afraid.

She did not know what to think.

"There must be witches in it," she said.

She went to the window to throw the pudding out. Just then a poor beggar was passing by the house.

"Here is a pudding you may have, if you like," said Tom's mother.

The beggar thanked her and put it into his basket.

He had not gone very far, when Tom got his head out of the pudding and shouted in a shrill voice, "Take me out! Take me out!"

The poor beggar was so frightened that he dropped his basket, pudding and all, and ran off as fast as he could.

Tom crawled out of the pudding, climbed out of the basket, and ran home.

His mother washed him and put him to bed.

Not long after this Tom's mother took him with her when she went to milk the cow.

That he might not get lost, she tied him to a wisp of hay.

When Tom's mother was not looking the cow took the wisp of hay into her mouth.

She began to chew and chew.

Tom began to jump about and shout.

He frightened the cow so that she opened her great mouth and out Tom jumped.

Then Tom's mother took him in her apron and ran with him to the house, but he was not hurt in the least.

One day Tom was in the field helping his father.

"Let me drive the horse home," said Tom.

"You drive the horse!" said his father.

"How could you hold the reins?"

"I could stand in the horse's ear and tell him which way to go," said Tom.

So his father put him in the horse's ear, and he drove safely home.

"Mother! Mother!" cried Tom.

But when Tom's mother came out, she could see no one. She began to be afraid.

"Where are you, Tom?" she cried.

"Here I am in the horse's ear. Please take me down," said Tom.

His mother lifted him gently down, kissed him, and gave him a blackberry for his supper.

Tom's father made him a whip out of a straw.

Tom tried to drive the cows, but he fell into a deep ditch.

There a great bird saw him and thought he was a mouse. The bird seized Tom in her claws and carried him towards her nest.

As they were passing over the sea, Tom got away and fell into the water, where a great fish swallowed him at one mouthful.

Soon after this the fish was caught, and it was such a big one that it was sent at once to King Arthur.

When the cook cut open the fish, out jumped Tom Thumb. Tom was brought before the king, and his story was told.

The king grew very fond of Tom and his wise sayings. He took Tom with him wherever he went.

If it began to rain, Tom would creep into the king's pocket and sleep until the rain was over.

The king had a new suit made for Tom, and gave him a needle for a sword.

A mouse was trained for Tom to ride.

The king and queen never tired of seeing him ride his queer little horse and bravely wave his sword.

One day, as they were going hunting, a cat jumped out and caught Tom's mouse.

Tom drew his sword and tried to drive the cat away.

The king ran to help poor Tom, but the little mouse was dead, and Tom was scratched and bitten.

Tom was put to bed, but he did not die.

No indeed! He was soon well again, and fought many brave battles and did many brave deeds to please the king.

CINDERELLA

Once upon a time there lived a maiden named Cinderella.

Her mother was dead, and she had to work very, very hard in the kitchen.

She had two older sisters, but they were unkind to little Cinderella. They made her stay among the pots and the kettles and do all the hard work about the house. Sometimes, to keep warm, she crept in among the cinders.

That is why she was called Cinderella.

One day the sisters came dancing into the house.

"We have been invited to the king's ball," they cried.

At length the day of the great ball came, and the two sisters rode away in their fine silk dresses.

Poor Cinderella, who had to stay behind, looked at her old ragged clothes, and burst into tears.

"Alas," she cried, "why should I always have to stay in the kitchen while my sisters dress in silks and satins?"

Hardly had she spoken when there stood before her a dear little old lady with a golden wand in her hand.

"My child," she cried, "I am your fairy god-mother, and you shall go to the ball, too.

"First go into the garden, Cinderella, and bring to me the largest pumpkin you can find."

When Cinderella had done this, the fairy waved her golden wand over the yellow pumpkin.

In a flash, it was not a pumpkin at all, but a beautiful yellow coach.

"Now bring me four white mice, two large ones and two small ones."

In a moment Cinderella brought a trap full of mice into the room.

The fairy waved her golden wand, and the two largest mice were turned into two snow-white horses.

The two small mice became two men, one a coachman, the other a footman.

"But how am I to go in these clothes?" said Cinderella.

"Ah, let me see," said the fairy, and she slowly waved her wand over the maiden's head.

Oh, what a change!

The rags tumbled to the floor. And, what do you think? In their place was a beautiful blue silk dress.

The ugly shoes fell off.

And, lo, a tiny pair of glass slippers were on Cinderella's little feet.

"Now listen to what I say," said the fairy godmother. "You must not stay after the clock strikes twelve.

"At that time your coach will again be a pumpkin, the men will be mice, and you will have on your old ragged dress."

Cinderella said she would not forget.

Then she jumped into the coach, and away she drove to the king's ball.

The king's son was charmed with Cinderella.

She was so very beautiful that he would dance with her and with no one else.

Cinderella had such a good time that she forgot about the clock.

It began to strike twelve—one, two, three . . .

Cinderella ran from the room. Down the steps of the palace she flew. She ran so fast that she lost one of her little glass slippers.

The clock finished striking.

Lo! The coach turned into a pumpkin.

The horses and men turned into mice.

Poor Cinderella had to walk home in her ragged clothes.

The next morning the prince found Cinderella's little glass slipper on the stairs.

"There is only one maiden in all the world who can wear so tiny a slipper," said the prince. "I will marry her and no other."

The prince hunted far and wide for a maiden who could put it on. Many tried, but none could do it.

At last he came to the house where Cinderella lived. The two elder sisters tried and tried to put the slipper on their large feet.

While the prince was waiting, Cinderella came into the room.

"Let me try it," she said.

"You!" cried the elder sisters. "You could never put it on."

"Let her try it," said the prince.

At once the little glass slipper was fitted to the tiny foot.

Then Cinderella stood up. Her ragged clothes turned into a beautiful silk dress, and there were two little slippers on her two little feet.

Then the prince knew that Cinderella was the one he had danced with at the ball, and taking her hand, he led her out to his coach.

Soon they were married and lived happily ever after

THE FOUR FRIENDS

music

Once upon a time a man had a donkey.

His donkey had worked for him many years.

At last the donkey grew so old that he was no longer of any use for work, and his master wished to get rid of him.

The donkey, fearing he might be killed, ran away.

He took the road to Bremen, where he had often heard the street band playing.

He liked music, so he thought he might join the band.

He had not gone far when he came upon an old dog.

The dog was panting, as if he had been running a long way.

"Why are you panting, my friend?" asked the donkey.

"Ah," said the dog, "I am too old for the hunt. My master wished to have me killed. So I ran away. But how I am to find bread and meat, I do not know."

"Well," said the donkey, "come with me. I am going to play in the band at Bremen. I think you and

I can easily earn a living by music. I can play the lute, and you can play the kettledrum."

The dog was quite willing, and so they both walked on.

They had not gone far when they saw a cat sitting in a yard.

He looked as sad as three days of rainy weather.

"What's the matter with you, old Tom?" asked the donkey.

"You would be sad, too," said the cat, "if you were in my place; for now that I am getting old and cannot catch mice, they wish to drown me. I have run away, but how I am going to live, I do not know."

"Come with us to Bremen," said the donkey. "We are going to play in the band.

"I know you love music, as you sing so well at night. You too can join the band."

"That is just what I should like to do," said the cat.

So the donkey, the dog, and the cat all walked on togeth

After a time the three came to a farmyard.

There on the gate sat a cock, crying "Cock-a-doddle-doo" with all his might.

"Why are you making so much noise?" asked the donkey.

"Ah," said the cock, "I find I must have my head cut off so that I may serve as a dinner for Monday. I'm crowing as hard as I can while my head is still on."

"Come with us, old Red Comb," said the donkey. "We are going to Bremen to join the band. You have a fine voice. You can join, too."

"Ah," said the cock, "that is just what I should like to do."

And they all went on their way to Bremen.

At evening the four friends came to a wood, where they stopped for the night.

The donkey and the dog lay down under a large tree.

The cat climbed up on one of the branches.

The cock flew to the very top of the tree, where he felt quite safe.

From his perch on the top of the tree the cock saw a light.

Calling to his friends, he said, "We are not far from a house. I can see a light."

"Let us go on," said the donkey, "for it may be just the house for us."

As they drew near, the light grew larger and brighter.

At last they could see that it came from the window of a robber's house.

The donkey, who was the tallest, went up and looked in.

"What do you see, old Long Ears?" asked the cock.

"What do I see?" answered the donkey. "Why, a table spread with plenty to eat and drink, and the robbers having their supper."

"We should be there, too, if we had our rights," said the cock.

"Ah, yes," said the donkey, "if we could only get inside."

Then the four friends talked over what they had better do in order to drive the robbers out of the house.

At last they hit upon a plan.

The donkey stood upon his hind legs and placed his front feet in the window sill.

The dog then stood on the donkey's back.

The cat climbed upon the dog, while the cock perched upon the cat's back.

The donkey gave a signal, and they began, all at the same time, to make their loudest music.

The donkey brayed, the dog barked, the cat mewed, and the cock crowed, all with such force that the window-pane shook and was almost broken.

The robbers had never heard such a noise.

They thought it must come from witches, or giants, or goblins, and they all ran as fast as they could to the wood behind the house.

Then our four friends rushed in and ate what the robbers had left upon the table.

It did not take long, for they ate as if they had been hungry for a month.

When the four had eaten, they put out the light, and each went to sleep in the spot which he liked the best.

The donkey lay down in the yard.

The dog lay behind the door.

The cat curled himself in front of the fire, while the cock flew up on a high beam.

They soon fell fast asleep.

When all was still and the light was out, the robber chief sent one of his bravest men back to the house. The man found the house quiet, so he went into the kitchen to strike a light.

Seeing the great fiery eyes of the cat, he thought they were live coals and held a match to them.

Puss was so angry that he flew up and scratched the man's face. This gave the robber a great fright, and he ran for the door.

As he went by, the dog sprang up and bit him in the leg.

In the yard the robber ran into the donkey, who gave him a great kick.

The cock on the beam was waked by the noise, and cried, "Cock-a-doodle-doo!"

The man ran as fast as his legs could carry him back to the robber chief.

"Ah!" he cried. "In that house is a wicked witch, who flew at me and scratched my face with her long nails.

By the door stood a man with a knife, who cut me in the leg.

Out in the yard lay a great black giant, who struck me a blow with his wooden club.

Upon the roof sat the judge, who cried, 'What did he do? What did he do?'

When I heard this I ran off as fast as I could."

The robbers never went near the house again.

The four friends liked the place so well that they would not leave it, and so far as I know, they are there to this day.

MOTHER FROST

daughters   heart   broad

At the edge of a wood there was a great, clear, bubbling spring of cold water.

Near this spring lived a widow with her daughter and her stepdaughter. The stepdaughter was very beautiful and a great help about the house, while the other girl was ugly and idle.

The mother loved only the ugly one, for she was her own child.

She cared so little for her stepdaughter that she made her do all the hard work.

Every day the poor girl would sit beside the spring and spin and spin, until her fingers bled.

One day, while she was washing the blood from her hands, the spindle fell into the spring and sank to the bottom. With tears in her eyes, she ran and told her stepmother what she had done.

The stepmother was angry and said, "You let the spindle fall into the spring. Now you must go and get it out."

The maiden went back to the spring to look for the spindle.

She leaned so far over the edge that her hand slipped, and down, down, she sank to the very bottom.

All at once she found that she was in a beautiful field where many wild flowers grew.

As she walked across the field, she came to a baker's oven full of new bread.

The loaves cried to her, "Oh, pull us out! Pull us out, or we shall burn!"

"Indeed I will!" cried the maiden.

Stepping up, she pulled all the sweet brown loaves out of the oven.

As she walked along, she came to a tree full of apples.

The tree cried, "Shake me! Shake me! My apples are all quite ripe!"

"Indeed I will!" cried the maiden.

So she shook the tree again and again, until there was not an apple left on its branches.

Then she picked up the apples, one by one, and piled them in a great heap.

When she had picked up all the apples, she walked on.

At last she came to a small house.

In the doorway sat an old woman who had such large teeth that the girl felt afraid of her and turned to run away.

Then the old woman cried, "What do you fear, my child? Come in and live here with me. If you will do the work about the house, I will be very kind to you. Only take care to make my bed well.

"You must shake it and pound it so that the feathers will fly about. Then the children down on the earth will say that snowflakes are falling, for I am Mother Frost."

The old woman spoke so kindly that she won the maiden's heart.

"I will gladly work for you," she said.

The girl did her work well, and each day she shook up the bed until the feathers flew about like snowflakes.

She was very happy with Mother Frost, who never spoke an angry word.

After the girl had stayed a long time with the kind old woman, she began to feel homesick.

She could not help it, though her life with Mother Frost had been so happy.

At length she said, "Dear Mother Frost, you have been very kind to me, but I should like to go home to my friends."

"I am pleased to hear you say that you wish to go home," said Mother Frost. "You have worked for me so well that I will show you the way myself".

She took the maiden by the hand and led her to a broad gateway.

The gate was open, and as she went through, a shower of gold fell over the maiden.

It clung to her clothes, so that she was dressed in gold from her head to her feet.

"That is your pay for having worked so hard," said the old woman. "And here is your spindle that fell into the spring."

Then the gate was closed, and the maiden found herself once more in the world.

She was not far from her own home, and as she came into the farmyard, a cock on the roof cried loudly,

"Cock-a-doodle-doo!

Our golden lady has come home, too."

When the stepmother saw the girl with her golden dress, she was kind to her. Then the maiden told how the gold had fallen upon her.

The mother could hardly wait to have her own child try her luck in the same way.

This time she made the idle daughter go to the spring and spin.

The lazy girl did not spin fast enough to make her fingers bleed.

So she pricked her finger with a thorn until a few drops of blood stained the spindle.

At once she let it drop into the water, and sprang in after it herself.

The ugly girl found herself in a beautiful field, just as her sister did.

She walked along the same path until she came to the baker's oven.

She heard the loaves, cry, "Pull us out! Pull us out, or we shall burn!"

But the lazy girl said to the brown loaves, "I will not. I do not want to soil my hands in your dirty oven."

Then she walked on until she came to the apple tree.

"Shake me! Shake me!" it cried, "for my apples are quite ripe."

"I will not," said the girl, "for some of your apples might fall on my head."

As she spoke, she walked lazily on.

At last the girl stood before the door of Mother Frost's house.

She had no fear of Mother Frost's great teeth, but walked right up to the old woman and offered to be her servant.

For a whole day the girl was very busy, and did everthing that she was told to do.

On the second day she began to be lazy, and on the third day she was still worse.

She would not get up in the morning.

The bed was never made, or shaken, so that the feathers could fly about.

At last mother Frost grew tired of her and told her that she must go away.

This was what the lazy girl wanted, for she felt sure that now she would have the golden shower.

Mother Frost led her to the great gate, but as she passed under it, a kettle full of black pitch was upset over her.

"That is what you get for your work," said the old woman, as she shut the gate.

The idle girl walked home, covered with pitch.

When she went into the farmyard the cock on the roof cried out,

"Cock-a-doodle-doo!

"Our sticky lady has come home, too."

The pitch stuck so fast to the girl that, as long as she lived, it never came off.

WHY THE BEAR'S TAIL IS SHORT

circus

Did you ever go to a circus where there was a bear in a cage? Did you notice how short his tail was? I will tell you how the bear's tail came to be short.

One very cold day in winter, a fox saw some men taking home a load of fish.

The fox jumped upon the wagon while the men were not looking. He drew off some of the best fish until he had enough for his dinner.

Then Mr. Fox jumped from the wagon and began to eat the fish.

While he was eating the fish, Mr. Bear came along.

"Good morning," said Mr. Bear, "you have had good luck fishing today. These are very fine fish. How did you catch them?"

"They are fine fish," said Mr. Fox. "If you will go fishing with me tonight, I will show you how to catch even better fish than these."

"I will go with you gladly," said the bear. "I will bring my hook and line too."

"You don't need a hook and line," said the fox.

"I always catch fish with my tail. You have a much longer tail than I, and can fish so much the better."

At sunset the bear met the fox.

They went across the frozen river until they came to a small hole in the ice.

"Now, Mr. Bear," said the fox, "sit down here on the ice and put your tail through the hole. You must keep still for a long while. That is the best way to catch fish.

"Wait until a great many fish take hold of your tail. Then pull with all your might."

The bear sat very still for a long time. At last he began to feel cold and he moved a little.

"Ow!" he cried, for his tail had begun to freeze in the ice.

"Is it not time to pull out the fish?" said the bear.

"Wait until more fish have taken hold of your tail. You are very strong. You can wait a little longer."

So the poor bear waited until it was almost morning.

Just then some dogs began to bark on the bank of the river.

The bear was so afraid that he jumped up quickly and pulled with all his might, but his tail was frozen fast in the ice.

He pulled and pulled until at length the tail was broken short off.

Mr. Fox ran away laughing and laughing at the trick he had played upon Mr. Bear.

Bears' tails have been short ever since.

RUMPELSTILTSKIN

chamber   promise   Melchior   precious

Once upon a time there lived a miller who had a beautiful daughter.

Now the miller had to visit the king's castle, and, while there, he happened to meet the king face to face.

The king stopped and spoke to the miller. The miller, wishing the king to think that he was very rich, told him that he had a daughter who could spin straw into gold.

"Ah," said the king, "that is indeed a wonderful gift. Tomorrow you must bring your daughter to my castle, that she may spin some gold for me."

Then the miller was afraid and wished he had not spoken, but he had to do as the king ordered. The next day he brought his daughter to the castle.

Now it happened that the king loved gold above all things.

So taking the poor girl by the hand, he led her into one of the great rooms of the castle.

There, in the middle of the room, stood a spinning wheel, and near it was a great heap of straw.

The king turned to the miller's daughter, and said,

"There is your spinning wheel, and here is the straw. If you do not spin all of it into gold by morning, your head shall be cut off."

Then the king left the room and locked the door behind him.

The poor girl could only sit and weep, for she had not the least idea how to spin straw into gold.

While she was crying, the door flew open and a little old man stepped into the room.

He had bandy legs, a long red nose, and wore a tall, peaked cap. Bowing low to the maiden, he said,

"Good evening, my dear young lady. Why are you crying?"

"Alas," said the girl, "the king has ordered me to spin all this staw into gold, and I do not know how."

Then the little man said, "What will you give me if I spin it for you?"

"This string of gold beads from my neck," said the girl.

The little man took the beads, and sitting down, began to spin.

Whir, whir, went the wheel; round and round it whirled.

Lo! As the maiden looked, she saw the coarse straw turn into beautiful golden threads.

The little man kept so busily at work that soon all the straw was gone, and in its place lay a heap of the finest gold.

The next morning the king unlocked the door. How his eyes sparkled at the sight of the gold!

These riches made the king even more greedy than before.

He led the maiden to a still larger chamber which was full of staw.

Turning to the trembling girl, he said, "There is your spinning wheel, and here is the straw. If you do not spin all of it into gold by morning, your head shall be cut off."

The maiden's eyes filled with tears at the sight of that huge heap of straw. Sitting down, she began to cry.

All at once the door opened and in jumped the little old man. He took off his pointed cap and said to the miller's daughter, "What will you give me if I help you again, and spin this straw into gold?"

"This ring from my finger," said the maiden.

The little man took the ring, and seating himself before the spinning wheel, began to spin.

Whir, whir, went the wheel. Faster and faster it whirled.

In the morning the straw had all been turned into finest gold.

When the king opened the door, how his eyes glistened at the sight of the gold! Still, it only made him greedy for more, so taking the poor girl by the hand, he led her to a much larger chamber.

This was so full of straw that there was hardly room for her to sit at the spinning wheel.

Turning the maiden, the king said,

"There is your spinning wheel, and here is the straw. If you do not spin all of it into gold by morning, your head shall be cut off. But if you do spin the gold, I will marry you and make you my queen."

"For," thought the king, "though she is only a miller's daughter, yet she can make me the richest king in the world."

Hardly had the door closed behind the king, when the little old man came hopping and skipping into the room.

Taking off his pointed cap, he said to the girl, "What will you give me if I again spin this straw for you?"

"Ah," said the maiden, "I have nothing more to give."

"Then you must make me a promise," said the little man. "You must promise to give me your first child, after you have become queen."

The poor girl saw no other way to save her life, so she gave her promise to the little man.

Then he sat down and began to spin.

Whir, whir, went the wheel. Faster and faster he spun.

Soon the great roomful of straw was all turned into gold.

When the king opened the door the next morning, he saw the maiden sitting beside a large heap of shining gold.

The king kept his promise, and made the poor miller's daughter his queen.

About a year later the queen had a lovely child, but she forgot all about her promise.

One day the little old man came hopping into the queen's room said, "Now give me what you have promised."

The queen was filled with terror, and offered the little man all the riches of the kingdom if he would leave her the child.

"No, I do not care for riches; you must keep your promise.

Then the queen began to mourn and to weep, until the little man had pity for her.

"I will give you three days," he said, "and if, in that time, you can guess my name, you shall keep the child."

The queen lay awake that night, thinking of all the names she had ever heard. In the morning men were sent to every part of the kingdom to find strange names.

The next day the little man came again. The queen began to call off to him all the names that she had found—Caspar, Melchior, and many, many others.

At each one the little man shook his head, and said, "No, that is not my name."

. Then the queen sent her man from house to house through the town. They took down the name of every man, woman, and child.

When the little man came again, the queen had a long list of names to give him.

"Is your name Cowribs, or Sheepshanks, or Bandylegs?" she said to him at last.

He answered to each one, "No, that is not my name."

On the third day the queen's men began to come back from all parts of the kingdom. They had been far and wide to find new names.

One of these men said, "I could not find any new names, but going by some deep woods, I heard a fox wish good-night to a rabbit.

"Soon I came upon a little house, in front of which a fire was burning. Round this fire danced a little man.

He wore a pointed cap, and had a long nose and bandy legs. As he went hopping and jumping about, first on leg and then on the other, he sang,

> "I'll bake tomorrow and brew today,
> And fetch the precious child away,
> For little knows her Royal Dame
> That Rumpelstiltskin is my name."

The queen clapped her hands for joy. She knew that at last she had found the name.

She sent the servant away with a bag of gold, and waited for the queer little man to come to her. At sunset the little fellow came hopping and skipping up to the queen.

"Now, O queen," he said, "this is your last chance. Tell me my name."

The queen asked, "Is your name Conrad?"
"No."
"Henry?"
"No."
"Then your name is Rumpelstiltskin."
"The fairies have told you!" shouted the little man, dancing about.

He became so angry that, in his rage, he stamped his right foot into the ground.

This made him more angry still, and taking hold of his left foot with both hands, he pulled so hard that he tore himself quite in two.

THE GOLDEN TOUCH

Midas   Marigold   creature   statue

Many years ago there lived a king named Midas.

King Midas had one little daughter, whose name was Marigold.

King Midas was very, very rich. It was said that he had more gold than any other king in the world.

One room of his great castle was almost filled with yellow gold pieces.

At last the king grew so fond of his gold that he loved it better than anything else in all the world.

He even loved it better than his own little daughter, dear little rosy-cheeked Marigold. His one great wish seemed to be far more and more gold.

One day while he was in his gold room counting his money, a beautiful fairy boy stood before him.

The boy's face shone with a wonderful light, and he had wings on his cap and wings on his feet. In his hand he carried a strange-looking wand, and the wand also had wings.

"Midas, you are the richest man in the world," said

the fairy. "There is no king who has so much gold as you."

"That may be," said the king. "As you see, I have this room full of gold, but I should like much more; for gold is the best and the most wonderful thing in the world."

"Are you sure?" asked the fairy.

"I am very sure," answered the king.

"If I should grant you one wish," said the fairy, "would you ask for more gold?"

"If I could have but one wish," said the king, "I would ask that everything I touch should turn to beautiful yellow gold."

"Your wish shall be granted," said the fairy.

"At sunrise tomorrow morning your slightest touch will turn everything into gold. But I warn you that your gift will not make you happy."

"I will take the risk," said the king.

The next morning King Midas awoke very early. He was eager to see if the fairy's promise had come true.

As soon as the sun rose he tried the gift by touching the bed lightly with his hand.

The bed turned to gold.

He touched the chair and table.

Upon the instant they were turned to solid gold.

The king was wild with joy.

He ran round the room, touching everything he could see. His magic gift turned all to shining, yellow gold.

The king soon felt hungry and went down to eat his breakfast. Now a strange thing happened. When he raised a glass of clear cold water to drink, it became solid gold.

Not a drop of water could pass his lips.
The bread turned to gold under his fingers.
The meat was hard, and yellow, and shiny.
Not a thing could he get to eat.
All was gold, gold, gold.

His little daughter came running in from the garden.

Of all living creatures she was the dearest to him.

He touched her hair with his lips.

At once the little girl was changed to a golden statue.

A great fear crept into the king's heart, sweeping all the joy out of his life.

In his grief he called and called upon the fairy who had given him the gift of the golden touch.

"O fairy," he begged, "take away this horrible golden gift. Take all my lands. Take all my gold. Take everything, only give me back my little daughter."

In a moment the beautiful fairy was standing before him.

"Do you still think that gold is the greatest thing in the world?" asked the fairy.

"No! no!" cried the king. "I hate the very sight of the yellow stuff."

"Are you sure that you no longer wish to have the golden touch?" asked the fairy.

"I have learned my lesson," said the king. "I no longer think gold the greatest thing in the world."

"Very well," said the fairy, "take this jug to the spring in the garden and fill it with water. Then sprinkle those things which you have touched and turned to gold."

The king took the jug and rushed to the spring. Running back, he first sprinkled the head of his dear little girl.

Instantly she became his own darling Marigold again, and gave him a kiss.

The king sprinkled the golden food, and to his great joy it turned back to real bread and real butter.

Then he and his little daughter sat down to breakfast. How good the cold water tasted! How eagerly the hungry king ate the bread and butter, the meat, and all the good food!

The king hated his golden touch so much that he sprinkled even the chairs and the tables and everything else the fairy's gift had turned to gold.

THE BELL OF ATRI

    justice   soldier   enough

Once upon a time a good and wise king ruled in the city of Atri.

He wished all his people to be happy.

In order that justice might be done to every one, he ordered a great bell to be hung in a tower.

Tied to the bell was a strong rope, so long that it reached nearly to the ground.

"I have placed the bell in the centre of my city," said the king, "so that it will be near all the people. The rope I have made long, so that even a little child can reach it."

Then the king gave out this order.

"If there be any one among my people who feels that he has not been justly treated, let him ring this bell. Then, whether he be old or young, rich or poor, his story shall be heard."

The bell of justice had hung in its place for may years.

Many times it had been rung by the poor and needy, and justice had been done to all who had asked for it.

At length the old rope became worn with use and age.

When it was taken down, another rope, long enough and strong enough, could not be found. So the king had to send away for one.

"What if some one should need help while the rope is down?" cried the people. "We must find something to take its place."

So one of the men cut a long grape-vine and fastened it to the great bell.

It was in the springtime, and green shoots and leaves hung from the grape-vine rope.

Near Atri, there lived a rich old soldier.

This soldier owned a horse that had been with him through many battles.

The horse had grown old and lame, and was no longer able to work.

So his cruel master turned him out into the streets to get his living as best he could.

"If you cannot find enough to eat, then you may die," said the cruel old man; "you are of no use to me."

The old horse went limping along; he grew thinner and thinner.

At length he limped up to the tower where the bell of justice hung.

His dim eyes saw the green shoots and the fresh leaves of the grape-vine.

Thinking they were good to eat, he gave a pull at the vine.

"Ding-dong! Ding-dong!" said the great bell. The people came running from the sides.

"Who is calling for justice?" they cried.

There stood the poor old horse, chewing the grape-vine.

"Ding-dong! Ding-dong!" rang the great bell.

"Whose horse is this?" asked the judges, as they came running up.

Then the story of the old horse was told.

The judge sent for his cruel master.

They ordered that he should build a warm barn, and that the faithful horse should have the best of hay and grain as long as he lived.

The people shouted for joy at this act of justice, but the cruel old man hung his head in shame and led the old horse away.

ESCAPE FROM RED INDIANS

    capture   tongue   ocean

Many years ago two boys lived on a farm in America. It was so long ago that there were few white people in that country.

The farms were scattered, and around them were great forests. The houses were made of logs, with strong, heavy doors.

Far away in the woods lived many Indians.

Sometimes the Indians would come down where the white people lived, and would capture any white person whom they could find.

They even dared to attack, and often burned, the scattered log cabins. The white prisoners would be taken to the Indian villages and would be held there as captives.

One cold winter morning the two brothers, John and William, were going skating on the river. In order to reach the river, they had to pass through some woods.

John, the elder brother, started first.

He threw his skates over his back and ran off whistling towards the river.

William, the younger brother, had to stay behind to fill with wood the huge box beside the fireplace.

Indians had not been seen near the farm for many years, so John was not in the least afraid.

As he went through the woods towards the river two huge Indians, with painted faces, jumped from behind trees where they had been hiding.

Before John could run he was caught, and his hands were tried behind his back.

Then they heard William shout as he ran down the path after his brother.

John knew that the Indians might kill him if he warned his brother. But he was brave, and before they could stop him, he cried out, "Indians! Indians!"

The Indians were angry and struck at John with their tomahawks. But he was not afraid; he faced the Indians bravely.

William heard the shout of warning, and ran like a deer back to the log cabin.

The heavy door was shut with a slam, and John's father, with his rifle, waited for the Indian attack.

But the two Indians did not dare attack the log cabin.

Dragging John after them, they started up the river bank towards their Indian town, many, many miles away.

All day long they travelled, and at night they built a small fire.

Over this fire they roasted a partridge which one of them had shot. John was given his share of the bird and a handful of parched Indian corn.

The Indians looked at John's skates, which still hung over his shoulder. They did not know what skates were. They thought they must be some of the white man's magic.

On and on they travelled for many days following an old Indian path.

All through the long march John still carried his skates.

At length they came to the Indian village.

Some of the Indian houses were long huts covered with strips of birch bark. Four or five families lived in each of these houses.

Other families lived in tents which they called 'teepees'.

John was given to an Indian woman who had lost her own boy the year before.

John's Indian mother was good to him, and treated him as if he were her own son.

Once the Indian boys thought they would test John's courage, so they formed in two lines, while each boy held a stout stick.

They they ordered John to run down between the two long lines. They had their sticks all ready to beat him. They thought John would be afraid and so would do as they told him.

But John was a strong lad, and jumping upon the first boy, he took his stick away from him.

Armed with this stick, John struck right and left at the heads of the boys until they were all glad to run away.

The Indian men liked to see John's courage, and laughed long and loud when the Indian boys ran away.

After this the boys were glad to let John play with them. With their bows and arrows they shot at a mark. They swam in the river and played games of tag, hide and seek, and ball.

In the spring the Indian women planted the yellow corn.

When the corn was up, the squaws went into the fields to hoe out the weeds. For a hoe they used a flat piece of stone tied to a wooden handle.

As John was a white boy the squaws tried to make him help hoe the corn.

When John took the hoe, he hoed up the corn and left the weeds. The angry squaws made signs to him that he must not do so.

Then John threw the hoe far from him.

"Hoeing is fit for squaws, not for warriors," he shouted. He had learned this from the Indian boys.

The old men were pleased. They thought John would make a fine warrior.

John had lived with the Indians a year.

He had learned to speak their tongue, but they did not trust him.

Some of them were always with him, for they were afraid he would run away.

All this time John had kept his skates carefully hidden.

One day the ice froze clear and smooth.

John brought his skates down to the river bank.

Many of the Indians followed to see what he was going to do.

They crowded around him on the ice.

John thought he would play a trick on them.

He strapped the skates upon the feet of an Indian boy.

The boy tried to stand up, but his feet slipped out from under him, and down he bumped upon the ice.

How the Indians laughed!

They thought it was a great joke.

Each of them in turn tried on the skates.

How they sprawled and fell upon the ice!

What fun it was for the other Indians!

When they were tired of the sport they held out the skates to John and asked him to put them on.

John strapped on the skates with great care.

He was a good skater, but he made believe that he could not skate at all.

He fell down and bumped his head.

He tripped over his toes and made great fun for the Indians.

They did not see that each time he fell he was a little farther out on the ice.

All at once John jumped up.

Away he flew, skating for his life.

Down the river he went, swift as a bird.

The Indians rushed after him, but he had too great a start.

The Indians were swift runners, but John, on his skates, was swifter still.

He knew that the river must flow towards the ocean, and that near the ocean lived the white people.

On and on he skated.

Two days later he saw the smoke of a white man's cabin and knew that he was safe.

John soon found his father and mother.

How glad they were to see him!

DICK WHITTINGTON

mayor   honest

Dick Whittington was a poor little boy who lived in the country. His father and mother were both dead.

Poor little Dick was always willing to work, but sometimes there was no work for him to do, so he often had nothing to eat.

Now Dick was a bright boy. He kept both ears open to hear what was said around him. He had heard many times about the great city of London.

Men said that in this great city the people were rich. Dick had even heard that the streets were paved with gold.

"How I should like to visit that great city," thought Dick, "for I could pick up gold from the streets."

Dick had earned a little money, so one day he set out to walk to London. He walked and walked and walked, but London was a long way from his home. At last a man with a cart came along. He was a kind man, and he gave Dick a ride.

"Where are you going?" asked Dick.

"I'm going to London," said the man.

"You are very good to give me a ride. I am going there, too," said Dick.

It was dark when they reached London.

That night Dick slept in a barn with the horses. The next morning he looked for the golden stones in the streets. He looked and looked, but he could find only dust and dirt.

There were many, many people in London, and Dick thought that he could soon find something to do. He wandered round the streets, seeking for work. He asked many people, but no one wanted the poor little country boy.

As Dick had no money for food, he soon became very, very hungry. At last he grew so weak that he fell down before the door of a great house. Here the cook found him and began to beat him with a stick.

"Run away, you lazy boy!" she cried.

Poor Dick tried to rise, but he was so faint from want of food that he could not stand.

Just then the owner of the house Mr. Fitzwarren, came up. He took pity on the poor boy and ordered the cook to give him some food.

Then he turned to Dick and said,

"If you wish to work, you may help the cook in the kitchen. You will find a bed in the attic."

Dick thanked Mr. Fitzwarren again and again for his kindness.

The cook was very unkind to Dick and whipped him almost every day. His bed in the attic was only a pile of old rags. He soon found that there were many rats and mice in the attic. They ran over his bed and made so much noise every night that he could not sleep.

"I wish I had a cat," thought Dick, "for she could eat up these rats and mice."

One day Dick earned a penny by blacking a man's shoes.

"I will try to buy a cat with this penny," thought Dick.

So he started out and soon met a woman with a large cat.

"Will you sell me that cat?" said Dick. "I will give you this penny for her."

"You are a good boy," said the woman, "and you may have the cat for a penny, for I know you will treat her kindly."

That night Dick's bed was free from rats, and Miss Puss had a good supper. Dick began to love his cat dearly.

Now Mr. Fitzwarren had many ships which sailed to distant lands. When a ship sailed, Mr. Fitzwarren let every one in his house send something on it. The things were sold, and when the ship came back, each person had the money for what he had sent.

One of the ships was ready to sail. Every one in the house except Dick had sent something.

"What is Dick going to send in the ship?" said Mr. Fitzwarren.

"Oh, that boy has nothing to send," said the cross cook.

"It is true," said poor Dick; "I have nothing but my dear cat."

"Well, then you must send your cat," said Mr. Fitzwarren.

How lonely poor Dick was without Puss!

The cook made fun of him for sending a cat on the ship.

At last Dick became so unhappy that the he made up his mind to run away. He started early in the morning, before any one in the house was up. He had gone but a short way when he heard the sound of the six great bells of Bow.

As they rang, "Ding-dong, ding-dong!" they seemed to say:

> Turn back, Whittington,
> Lord Mayor of London.

"It is strange that the bells should speak to me," said Dick, "but if I am to be Lord Mayor of London, I will gladly turn back."

So he ran back to the house of Mr. Fitzwarren.

"I hope they have not missed me," said Dick, as he gently opened the door and stole softly in.

Dick's cat was taken across the ocean.

The ship sailed and sailed, until at last it came to a distant country.

Now the king and queen of this country were very rich. When the captain was asked to show his goods before them he was very glad indeed to do so. The king and queen first gave the captain a great feast. Gold and silver dishes filled with food were brought in.

When these dishes were placed upon the table an army of rats came out. There were white rats, and black rats, and brown rats, and big rats, and little rats. At once they fell upon the food and ate it nearly all up.

"Why do you let the rats do this?" asked the captain.

"Alas, we cannot help ourselves," said the king. "I would give half my kingdom to be rid of them."

Then the captain thought of Dick Whittington's cat. "I have an animal which will rid you of them," said the captain.

"Pray bring it in at once," said the queen.

What fun Dick's cat had killing the rats and mice in the king's palace!

"We must buy that little animal," said the queen. "I do not care how much she may cost."

The captain could hardly carry all the jewels and gold that the king gave him for the cat.

Then the ship with Dick's money came back to London, and the captain told the story to Mr. Fitzwarren.

"We must take these jewels and all this gold at once to Mr. Whittington," said the honest man. "He is no longer a poor boy, for this has made him rich."

They found Dick in the kitchen blacking the stove.

"Come with me at once into the parlour," said Mr. Fitzwarren.

Then the bags of gold and jewels were piled at Dick's feet.

"See what your cat has brought you," said Mr. Fitzwarren. "You are now a rich man and may yet be Lord Mayor of London."

And it is true that after Dick Whittington became a man, he was made Lord Mayor of London.

BRIAR ROSE

honour

A long time ago there lived a king and queen who longed to have a child.

One day, when the queen was resting near a spring, a frog crept out of the water and said to her, "You shall have your wish. Within a year you shall have a little girl."

What the frog said came true. The queen had a child who was so beautiful that the king gave a party in her honour. He wished to invite all the wise women in the land, for these wise women could grant fairy gifts to his little child. There were thirteen of them, but only twelve were invited, as the king had only twelve golden plates.

After the dinner was over, the wise women in turn rose from the table and named their fairy gifts to the little princess. The first gave to her goodness; the second, beauty; the third, riches; and so on, up to the last.

Before the twelfth wise woman could speak, in walked the thirteenth. This woman was in a great rage because she had not been invited.

She cried in a loud voice, "When the princess is fifteen years old she shall prick her finger with a spindle and shall fall down dead."

At these words every one turned pale with fright. The twelfth wise woman, who had not yet spoken, now came up and said, "I could not stop this woman's evil words. I can only make them less harsh. The king's child shall not die, but a deep sleep shall fall upon her, in which she shall stay one hundred years."

The little princess was so beautiful, so kind, and so good that no one who knew her could help loving her. As she grew older the king and queen began to feel very unhappy, for they could not help thinking of what was to happen to their dear little daughter. They ordered all the spindles in the kingdom to be burned.

Now, as it happened, on the very day that the princess was fifteen years old, the king and queen were away from home. The princess was quite alone in the castle, and she ran all over the palace, looking in at rooms and halls, just as her fancy led her.

At last she came to an old tower at the top of a winding stair. She saw a little door. In the lock was a rusty key. When she turned it, the door flew open. There, in a small room, sat an old woman with her spindle, spinning flax.

"Good morning," said the princess. "Do tell me what that funny thing is that jumps about so." And then she held out her hand to take the spindle. It came about just as the fairy had foretold.

The princess pricked her finger with the spindle. At once she fell upon a bed which was near, and lay in a deep sleep as if dead.

This sleep came not only upon the princess, but spread over the whole castle.

The king and queen, who had just come home, fell asleep, and all the their lords and ladies with them. The horses went to sleep in the stable; the dogs in the yard; the doves on the roof; the flies on the wall; yes, even the fire that burned in the fireplace grew still and slept.

The meat stopped roasting before the fire.

The cook in the kitchen was just going to box the ears of the kitchen boy, but her hand dropped and she sank to sleep.

Outside the castle the wind was still, and upon the trees not a leaf stirred.

In a short time there sprang up round the castle a hedge of thorn bushes. Year by year the hedge grew higher and higher, until at last nothing of the castle could be seen above it, not even the roof, nor the chimneys, nor the flag on the tower.

As years went by the story of the sleeping beauty was told all over the kingdom. Many kings' sons came and tried to get through the hedge of thorns, but this they could not do. The sharp thorns seemed to have hands which held the young men fast.

After many, many years a prince came from a far-off kingdom. He heard the story of the castle and its sleeping beauty. He knew what danger lay in the great hedge of thorn bushes. But the young prince was brave, and he was not to be turned back.

"I am not afraid. I will go out and seek this beautiful Briar Rose," he said.

It happened that the hundred years of the magic spell had just ended. The day had come when the sleeping princess was to wake up again.

As the prince came to the hedge of thorn bushes, it was in full bloom and covered with beautiful red flowers. There, through the thorn bushes, lay a wide road.

Soon the prince came to the gates of the castle. He found the horses and dogs lying asleep on the ground. The doves sat on the roof with their heads under their wings.

He went into the castle. Even the flies on the wall still slept. Near the throne lay the king and queen, while all around were the sleeping lords and ladies. The whole castle was so still that he could hear his heart beat.

The prince went on from room to room until he came to the old tower. Going up the winding stair he saw the little door. A rusty key was in the lock, and the door was half open. There before him lay the sleeping princess.

The prince bent down and gave her a kiss. As he did so the sleeping beauty opened her eyes. With her the whole castle awoke.

The king awoke, and the queen, and all the lords and ladies.

The horses in the stable stood up and shook themselves. The dogs jumped about and wagged their tails. The doves on the roofs lifted their heads and flew into the fields.

The flies on the wall began to buzz.

The fire in the kitchen began to burn.

The meat began to roast.

The cook boxed the ears of the kitchen boy, so that he ran off crying.

The hedge of thorn bushes round the castle dried up and blew away.

Then the prince married the beautiful princess, and they lived happily ever after.

THE BAKER BOYS AND THE BEES

Andernach   guarded

Long years ago many cities had great stone walls round them. The walls were built to keep out enemies, for in those old days cities often went to war with one another.

The city of Andernach had round it one of these great walls. There was only one gateway into the city, and this gateway was guarded by strong iron doors.

Just behind the doors lived a gatekeeper, who did nothing but open and shut the gates. He watched them well. No one could come in who was not friendly to the city.

The gates were not opened very often. Some days they were not opened at all. So the gate-keeper had much spare time.

"I am very fond of honey," thought he. "I think I will buy a few hives of bees. I can place the hives on the top of the wall. There nobody will trouble them."

Soon there were rows of beehives, on the top of the wall over the gate.

It happened that, not far away, there was another walled city, named Lintz. The people of Lintz were the enemies of the people of Andernach.

They were always watching each other, and fought when they could get a chance.

Now the people of Lintz planned to attack and capture the city of Andernach. They called their wisest men together to see how the attack should be made. Many plans were talked over.

At length an old man said, "Men of Lintz, you know that the men of Andernach are lazy. They like to lie late in their beds. If we attack the city at sunrise, we shall capture it before they can get their eyes open."

This plan seemed wise to the people of Lintz, and an army was soon ready to march against the city of Andernach.

One dark night the army crept softly towards the walls of the sleeping city.

The only people who rose early in Andernach were the bakers. They had to have fresh bread ready for breakfast.

After their work was done the bakers used to have a morning nap, but the baker boys had to stay awake and watch the loaves of bread. Two of these boys, named Hans and Fritz, were fast friends and were always together.

One morning, just at sunrise, Hans said to Fritz, "Let us creep upon the wall over the gatekeeper's house. I think we can find some honey. The old gatekeeper is asleep; he will not hear us."

The two boys crept softly up the stairs. They soon reached the top of the wall.

"Did you hear that noise?" whispered Fritz.

"Yes, it must be the old gatekeeper," said Hans, in a low voice.

"No, it seems to come from over the wall," said Fritz.

The two boys crawled to the edge of the wall and carefully looked over.

There stood the army of Lintz. A ladder was placed against the wall. The solidiers would soon mount over the gate into the city.

What was to be done?

There was no time to wake the people.
What could two boys do against an army?
In an instant Fritz thought of the beehives.
Ah, the bees were awake if the people were not!
Each boy seized a hive and bore it carefully to the edge of the wall. Then with a strong push down tumbled hives, honey, and bees upon the heads of the enemy.

Such buzzing, such stinging, such shouting arose!

The boys ran down the stairs to the city hall.

The old bell-ringer was aroused by the cries.

Soon the wild clang of the bell awoke the people of Andernach.

Armed men ran to the city gate, but the bees had done their work well. There was no need for soldiers.

The army of Lintz was running away.

Over the great gate the people of Andernach placed a statue of the two baker boys whose quick wit had saved the city.

THE FIRST WIFE'S WEDDING RING

    heirs   heritage   comrade
               heyday!   decided

Many years ago there lived a worthy man who had married twice. By his wife he had a son, who soon after his mother's death decided to become a soldier and to travel far and wide. "When one has seen the world, one values home the more," said he, "and if I live I shall return."

So the father gave him his blessing, and his mother's wedding ring, saying, "Keep this ring, and then, however long you stay away, and however changed you may become, by this ring I shall know you to be my true son and heir."

In a short time the father married again, and by this marriage also he had one son.

Years passed by, and the elder brother did not return, and at last everyone believed him to be dead. But he was not dead, and after a long time he turned his steps homewards. He was so much changed by age and travelling that only his mother would have known him again, but he had the ring tied safe and fast round his neck. One night, however, he was too far from shelter to get a bed, so he slept under a hedge, and when he woke in the morning the string was untied and the ring was gone. He spent a whole day looking for it, but in vain; and last he decided to go on and explain the matter to his father.

The old man was overjoyed to see him and fully believed his tale, but with the second wife it was otherwise.

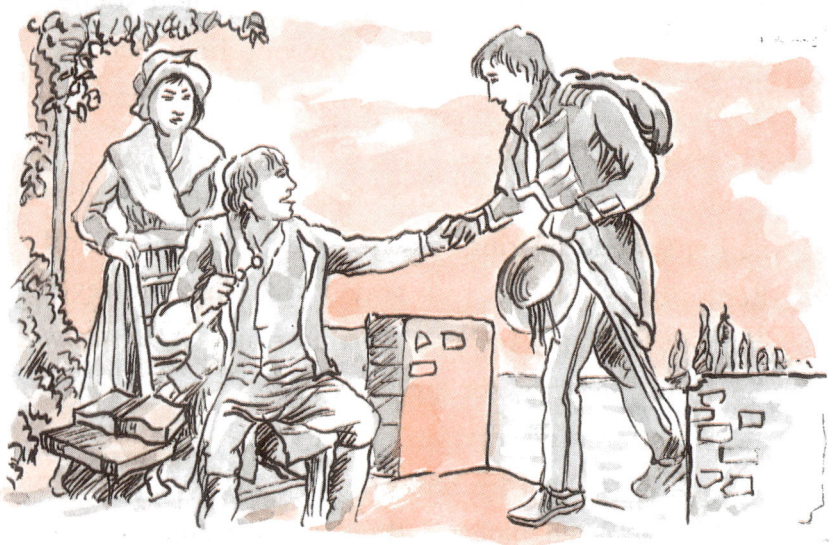

She was far from pleased to think that her child was not now to be the sole heir of his father's goods; and she so worked upon the old man by unkind and spiteful talk that he agreed to send away the newcomer till he should have found the first wife's wedding ring.

"Is the home I have taken such care of," she cried, "to go to the first wanderer who comes in with a brown face and a ragged coat, pretending that he is your son?"

So the soldier was sent wandering again, but his father followed him to the gate, and slipped some money into his hand, saying, "God speed you back again with the ring!"

It was Sunday morning, and the church bells were ringing as he turned sadly away.

"Ding-dong!" rang the bells, "Ding-dong! Why are you not dressed in your Sunday clothes, and wherefore do you heave such doleful sighs, whilst we ring so merrily? Ding-dong ! Ding-dong!"

"Is there not a cause?" replied the solidier. "This day I am turned out of home and heritage, though indeed I am the true heir."

"Nethereless we shall ring for your return," said the bells.

As he went, the sun shone on the green fields and in the soldier's eyes, and said, "See how brightly I shine! But you, comrade, why is your face so cloudy?"

"Is there not good reason?" said he. "This day I am turned out of home and heritage, and yet I am the true heir."

"Nethertheless I shall shine on your return," said the sun.

Along the road the hawthorn hedges were white with blossom. "Heyday!" they cried, "Who is this that comes trimp, tramp, with a face as long as a poplar tree? Cheer up, friend! It is spring, sweet spring! All is now full of hope and joy, and why should you look so doleful?"

"May I not be excused?" said the soldier. "This day I am turned out of home and heritage, and yet I am the true heir."

"Nevertheless we shall blossom when you return," said the hedge.

When he had wandered for three days and three nights, all he had was spent, and there was no shelter to be seen but a dark gloomy forest, which stretched before him. Just then he saw a small, wizened old woman, who was trying to lift a bundle of sticks on her back.

"That is too heavy for you, good mother," said the soldier; and he raised the bundle and settled it on her back.

"Have you just come here?" muttered the old woman; "then the best thanks I can give you is to bid you get away as fast as you can."

"I never retreated yet, dame," said the soldier, and on he went.

Presently he met with a giant, who was strolling along by the edge of the wood, knocking the cones off the tops of the fir-trees with his finger-nails. He was an ugly-looking monster, but he said civilly enough, "You look in want of employment, comrade. Will you take service with me?"

"I must first know two things," answered the soldier; "my work and my wages."

"Your work," said the giant, "is to cut a path through this wood to the other side. But then you shall have a year and a day to do it in.

"If you do it within the time, you will find at the other end a magpie's nest, in which is the ring you are seeking. The nest also contains the crown jewels which have been stolen, and if you take these to the king, you will need no further reward. But, on the other hand, if the work is not done within the time, you will for ever after be my servant without wages."

"You are a hard taskmaster," said the soldier, "but need knows no law, and I agree to your terms."

When he came into the giant's abode, he was greatly surprised to see the little wizened old woman. She showed no sign that they had met before, however, nor did the soldier show any sign that he recognized her. He soon found out that she was the giant's wife and much in dread of her husband, who treated her cruelly.

"Tomorrow you shall begin to work," said the giant.

"If you please," said the soldier, and before he went to bed he carried in water and wood for the old woman.

"There's a friendship in trouble," said he.

Next morning the giant led him to a spot on the outskirts of the forest, and giving him an axe, said, "The sooner you begin, the better, and you may see that it is not difficult." Saying which, he took hold of one of the trees by the middle, and snapped it off as one might pluck a flower.

"This is to thee, but how to me?" said the soldier; and when the giant went away he set to work. But through he was so strong, and worked willingly, the trees seemed almost as hard as stone, and he made little progress. When he returned at night the giant asked him how he got on.

"The trees are very hard," said he.

"So they always say," replied the giant; "I have always had lazy servants."

"I will not be called idle a second time," thought the soldier, and next day he went early and worked his utmost. But the result was very small. And when he came home, looking tired and disappointed, he could not help seeing that this pleased the giant.

Matters had gone on thus for some time, when one morning as he went to work he found the little old woman gathering sticks as before.

"Listen," said she. "He shall not treat you as he has treated others. Count seventy to the left from where you are working, and begin again. But do not let him know that you have made a fresh start. And do a little at the old place from time to time, as a blind."

Before he could thank her the old woman was gone. Without more ado he counted seventy from the old place, and hit the seventieth tree such a blow with his axe, that it came crashing down then and there. And he found that, one after another, the trees yielded to his blows as if they were touchwood. He did a good day's work, gave a few strokes in the old spot, and came home, taking care to look as gloomy as before.

Day by day he got deeper and deeper into the wood, the trees falling before him like dry elder twigs; and now the hardest part of his work was walking backwards and forwards to the giant's home, for the forest seemed to stretch on and on for ever. But on the three hundred and sixty-sixth day from his first meeting with the giant, the soldier cut fairly through on to an open plain, and as the light streamed in, a magpie

flew away. On searching her nest, the soldier found his mother's wedding ring. He also found many precious stones of priceless value, which were without a doubt the lost crown jewels. And as his year and a day of service with the giant were now ended, he did not trouble himself to return, but with the ring and the jewels in his pocket set off to find his way to the city.

He soon fell in with a good comrade who showed him the way, and pointed out everything of interest on the road. As they drew near, one of the royal carraiges was driving out of the city gates, in which sat three beautiful princesses who were the king's daughters.

"The two eldest are going to marry two princes," said the friend.

"And whom is the youngest to marry?" asked the soldier, "for she is by far the most beautiful."

"She will never marry," his friend replied, "for she is pledged to the man who shall find the crown jewels, and cut a path through the stonewood forest that borders her father's kingdom. And that is much as if she were promised to the man who should fetch down the moon for her to play with. For the jewels are lost beyond recall, and the wood is an enchanted forest."

"Nevertheless she shall be wed with my mother's wedding ring," thought the soldier. But he kept this to himself, and only waited until he had smartened himself up, before he begged to be taken to the king.

His claim to the princess was made good. The king heaped honours and riches upon him, and the princess whom he was to marry liked him so much that the wedding was fixed for an early day.

"May I bring my old father, madam?" he asked the princess.

"That you surely may," said she. "A good son makes a good husband."

As he entered his own village the hedges were in blossom, the sun shone and the bells rang for his return.

His stepmother now welcomed him, and was very eager to go to court also. But her husband said, "No, You took such good care of the home, it is but fit you should look to it whilst I am away."

As to the giant, when he found that he had been outwitted, he went off, and was never more heard of in those parts. But the soldier took the wizened old woman into the city and cared for her to the day of her death.

DAVID AND GOLIATH

Israel   Philistines   Goliath   forehead

Long, long ago there lived in the country of Israel a boy named David.

He was a shepherd boy, and all day long he watched the quiet sheep as they ate sweet grass on the hillside.

Although David was only a boy, he was tall and strong and brave. When he knew he was in the right, he feared nothing.

David's quiet life did not last long.

There was a great war between the people of Israel and men called the Philistines. All the strong men in David's town went to join the army of Israel. David could not go, as he had to tend the sheep, but his three elder brothers went to the war.

For a long time David's father heard nothing from his three eldest boys.

At length he called David to him and said, "Take to your brothers a bag of this corn and these ten loaves of bread. Find out how your brothers are, and bring word to me."

The next morning David rose very early, and taking the bag of corn and the loaves of bread, he went to the camp where his brothers were.

The camp of Israel was on the side of a high mountain. Across the valley from this mountain and on the side of another mountain was the camp of the Philistines.

After David had come to the camp and had found his brothers, shouts of anger and fear came from the soldiers.

David looked across the valley to the camp of the Philistines. There he saw a huge solidier dressed in shining armour.

This giant soldier carried a great spear and shield. "Who is that man?" asked David.

"Do you not know? That is Goliath," said the soldiers. "Every day he comes out and dares any man or our side to meet him in battle."

"Does no one of our soldiers dare to meet him?" asked David.

"We have no man so strong as he in our whole army," said the soldiers.

The giant from the opposite hillside shouted with a loud voice, and again dared the army of Israel to choose a man to meet him.

David was stirred to anger. "Is not God on our side?" he asked. "I will fight this man, even though he kill me."

The king of Israel heard of these brave words and sent for David to come before him.

When he saw that David was only a boy, he said, "You are not able to go against this Philistine. You are only a boy, while he has fought in many battles."

Then David said to the king, "Once, when I was guarding my father's sheep, I killed a lion and a bear without help from any one but the Lord. He will help me fight this man."

Then the king said, "Go, and the Lord be with you."

The king fitted David with heavy armour and gave to him his own sword, but David said, "I am not used to his heavy armour; it will only hinder me."

So he threw it off.

Then David went to a brook near by and chose five smooth stones.

Armed with these five stones and his sling, he went bravely out to meet the giant.

When the giant saw that David was only a boy, he was angry and cried out,

"Do you dare fight with me? I will kill you, and will give your flesh to the birds and the beasts."

David looked at him without fear and said, "You come against me with a sword and with a spear and with a shield, but I come to you in the name of the Lord. This day will He give you into my hand. I will kill you and take your head from you, and I will give the bodies of the Philistines to the birds and the beasts.

When they came near to each other, David fitted one of the five stones to his sling.

He whirled the sling swiftly about his head.

The stone flew straight to its mark.

It struck the Philistine full in the forehead.

The huge giant took one step and, with a groan, fell to the earth.

Then David, standing upon the giant, took his sword and cut off the head of his enemy.

When the Philistines saw that their giant was dead, they were filled with fear.

They left their camp and tried to run away, but the army of Israel followed them and won a great victory.

For this brave deed David was made a captain and was held in honour by the king.

PHONIC GROUP TABLES
and
PRONUNCIATION EXERCISES

The carefully classified Phonic Group Tables, which have been so important a feature of the Beacon course from the Preparatory Stage onward, reach their conclusion in the nine new tables on pages 137-140 of this book. These are followed by some useful Pronunciation Exercises which, used for a few minutes daily, will have a beneficial effect on the pupil's speech, spelling and powers of quick and accurate word recognition. The exercises give opportunity for the revision of many words used for the first time in the stories of *Briar Rose* and for the introduction of words having vowel and vowel-consonant sounds which are outside the scope of formal Phonic Group Tables, but whose correct pronunciation is necessary for accurate reading. As words of this type are introduced in the stories of *William Tell* (Book Six Stage of Beacon Reading), there is everything to be said in favour of the preliminary encounter at the Book Five Stage which these Pronuniciation Exercises afford.

PHONIC GROUP TABLES

Note: Phonic Tables LVI-LVII continue (from Book Four Stage) the study of silent letter words.

Group LVI. Silent *l* words.

half	calf	palm	calm	balm
stalk	walk	chalk	talk	folk

Group LVII. Silent *g* words.

gnat	gnome	gnaw	campaign	design
gnu	gnarled	gnash	sigh	reign

Revision table for Phonic Groups LI-LVII

climb	knee	sight	bought	often
comb	kneel	lighted	ought	soften
crumb	knelt	fright	sought	castle
dumb	knell	tightly	brought	jostle
lamb	knit	bright	fought	rustle
doubt	knife	thigh	caught	thistle
debt	knot	knight	naughty	whistle
limb	knock	right	daughter	chestnut
numb	knob	might	taught	fasten
thumb	know	night	slaughter	listen
folks	gnaw	wrap	alight	climber
chalk	gnu	wring	tonight	lambkin
talk	gnashed	wrung	crumbs	doubtful
walk	gnarled	wrong	dumb	knitting
stalk	gnomes	write	Newcastle	weighed

137

calf	gnat	wrapped	brightly	wrote
calves	sign	talking	written	thought
half	reign	reigned	walking	brought
halves	deign	frightened	talking	fighting
calm	feign	brightened	sighing	kneading

Group LVIII. In the following words *ie* and *ei* have the long sound of *e*.

field	priest	seize	fiend	wield
grief	yield	ceiling	piece	shield
brief	chief	receive	thief	relief
grieve	belief	receipt	frieze	believe
niece	siege	deceive	shriek	thieves

Groups LIX. In the following words *o* and *ou* have the short sound of *u*.

mother	honey	nothing	come	courage
comfort	company	wonderful	mongrel	country
money	London	oven	son	colour
love	some	front	lovely	trouble
kingdom	Monday	month	armour	couple
comfit	double	govern	young	cousin

Group LX. In the following words the *a* has the sound of short *o*.

was	wand	what	warrior	quantity
wasp	swan	wash	watch	quarrel
wanted	swallow	warren	swamp	quality
waffle	waddle	waddling	waft	squash
wadding	want	wander	washer	squat

Group LXI. In the following words the *w* sound modifies *ar* which has the sound of *or*.

warn	warm	warden	warp	warble
warned	sward	war	wardrobe	warder
swarm	reward	warship	warming	quart

Group LXII. In the following words *ph* is sounded like *f*.

photograph	asphalt	sulphur	gramophone
phlox	prophet	dolphin	paragraph
physics	typhoid	symphony	triumph
phantom	telephone	orphan	nymph
phial	elephant	pamphlet	lymph
Pharisee	alphabet	emphasize	telegraph
phrase	nephew	semaphore	autograph

Group LXIII. In the following words the two vowels together are sounded separately.

fuel	poem	giant	truant	duel
poet	idea	gruel	cruel	suet
diet	real	trial	Indian	dial
quiet	really	fiery	liar	piano
quietly	dais	fiat	friar	crier
bias	briar	drier	diadem	client
vial	violet	violent	India	diamond
kiosk	genius	idiot	radio	triangle
flier	usual	shoer	area	violin
sepia	viola	folio	fiord	lion
doer	goer	Noel	riot	rio

Groups LXIV. The suffixes *tion* and *sion* have the pronunciation *shun.*

nation	pension	motion	election
ration	division	protection	traction
option	infusion	detection	prevention
affection	permission	addition	station
admission	fraction	tension	intention
omission	notion	mission	session
mansion	friction	passion	collision

PRONUNCIATION EXERCISES

Exercise 1. The correct pronunciation of *wh* is important. In reality the *h* is sounded before the *w*, and in the oldest English words it was so written.

whit	whet	whig	whip	whiff
whistle	whisper	whirl	whimper	whether
whist	whim	which	whisk	when
white	whir	where	wheat	wheel

Exercise 2. K and *ck* are sounded exactly alike. Their use is not so confusing from the point of view of sounding as from spelling. The use of the *ck* after a short vowel should be emphasized.

rake	stake	peak	duck	croak
rack	stack	peck	duke	crock
lake	dike	speak	coke	cloak
lack	Dick	speck	cock	clock
lick	back	pick	pack	quick
like	bake	pike	bike	quake

Exercise 3. Tch generally has the same sound as *ch*, and usually follows vowels having the short sound.

each	teach	peach	reach	speech
bleach	screech	leech	breach	touch
coach	roach	poach	broach	which
fetch	stretch	itch	watch	much
blotch	catch	sketch	crutch	such
latch	batch	snatch	ditch	church
hatch	patch	hutch	twitch	search
switch	witch	stitch	scratch	match
hitch	birch	flitch	preach	clutch
Dutch	beach	approach	perch	leech

Exercise 4. This table practises the two sounds of *th*, so often mispronounced. (*Cf. Phonic Group Table IX-Book One Stage*).

fifth	tenth	stength	thud	thin
thing	thump	thick	thank	thatch
throb	throne	thrust	thrash	thrush
this	thus	these	those	that
them	than	then	the	thee
thy	bathe	lathe	seethe	tithe
blithe	lithe	clothe	scathe	thine
breathe	soothe	smooth	thence	sheathe

Exercise 5. A table of words containing the more common prefixes used in the vocabulary of *Briar Rose*.

awake	against	almost	before	because
about	agree	already	behind	circus
above	among	although	between	circle
across	alive	begin	beneath	circular
afraid	around	believe	beyond	circulate

content	command	discord	excused
contains	complete	decided	enjoy
concert	compete	defend	enchant
connect	distant	defer	enough
continue	dismiss	explain	enemies
comrade	disappoint	except	enlarge
compose	displease	extend	enable
forget	foreman	instant	outgoing
forsake	foremost	intrude	overflow
forwards	forecast	outside	overtook
forbid	income	outskirts	overjoyed
forgive	inside	outwitted	overcome
foresee	instead	outrun	overturn
foretold	indeed	outlook	overlays
prefer	return	retreated	untied
pretend	reward	repair	under
programme	recite	unkind	underneath
progress	recall	unlocked	undertake
protect	replied	unhappy	understand
reply	returned	undone	underfed
result	rejoined	untruth	underdone

Exercise 6. A table of words containing the more common suffixes in the vocabulary of *Briar Rose*.

cottage	mountain	local	peasant
courage	curtain	mortal	nobody
heritage	animal	distant	anybody
village	signal	instant	somebody
carriage	royal	servant	busybody
captain	naval	pleasant	everybody
church	stitch	cock	counted
coach	pitch	attack	decided
march	fetch	glistened	planted
touch	stuck	frightened	yielded
rich	trick	answered	guarded
watch	black	covered	banded
witch	sack	replied	posted

jewel	maiden	father	princess
cruel	wooden	stitches	duchess
travel	stolen	judges	countess
fuel	brother	witches	tigress
duel	daughter	horses	progress
frozen	sister	branches	express
listen	mother	marches	excess

dearest	locket	rustic	beautiful
wisest	socket	justice	doleful
smallest	jacket	notice	handful
youngest	attic	service	wonderful
loudest	music	practice	mouthful
basket	magic	apprentice	armful
pocket	garlic	crevice	thoughtful

goblin	visit	precious	blossom
satin	enormous	delicious	kingdom
rabbit	famous	luscious	dukedom

employment	kindness	outside	centre
enchantment	capture	beside	sceptre
goodness	creature	inside	spectre

cities	brewing	people	quietly
fairies	buzzing	priceless	gently
enemies	gentle	nevertheless	brightly
baking	castle	friendless	nightly

almost	lesson	parlour	angry
utmost	London	arrow	hungry
foremost	armour	fellow	country
reason	honour	window	pantry

upset	length	something	beauty
sunset	fourth	backward	cloudy
outset	anything	forward	gloomy
fifth	nothing	homeward	moody

WHAT COMES NEXT?

Old people, and young people as well, sometimes feel a little sad when they come to the end of a book which they have enjoyed reading. But there is no reason why should feel sad to have reached the end of *Briar Rose*. Your reading is now so good that for you anything and everthing is possible for 'What comes next?'

At the next stage in the Beacon series comes *William Tell*, another collection of stories, some of them may be old favourites and some of them quite new. You are sure to enjoy reading them.